HOW PREPARE A MUMMY

BY JILLIAN POWELL

CONTENTS

YOU WILL NEED

✓ A SHARP FLINT KNIFE

✓ NILE WATER

✓ A LONG-HANDLED HOOK

✓ A BODY THAT IS READY
FOR THE AFTER LIFE

✓ SOME PALM OIL

✓ SPONGES

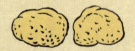

Undress the body and put it on a table which is sloping and has wooden slats.

Shave off the hair, then wash the body with the **Nile water** and the **palm oil**.

Now remove the insides of the body. Take everything out except the heart. (The spirit needs the heart in the After Life.)

Use the long-handled hook to pull the brains out through the nose.

MAKE THE CANOPIC

For the next stage, you will need four canopic jars: one jar to store the stomach, one for the liver, one for the lungs and one for the intestines.

Make the jars from clay and then use the paints to write magic spells on them. The spells will keep the contents safe.

YOU WILL NEED

✓ **CLAY TO MAKE JARS**

✓ **PAINTS**

✓ **BRUSHES**

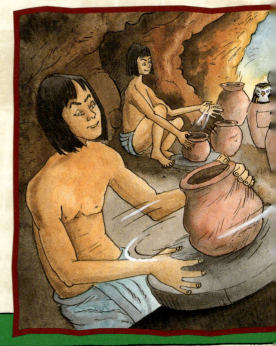

The jars need stoppers to go on top.

Make a baboon head stopper to look after the lungs,

a jackal to look after the stomach,

a falcon for the intestines

and a human head for the liver.

These stoppers represent the sons of Horus, the god of the rising sun. They will keep the body parts safe and prevent people using them to cast spells against the spirit.

PREPARE THE INSIDES

YOU WILL NEED

✓ NATRON SALT 　　✓ RESIN 　　✓ LINEN

Now prepare the insides of the body
to go into the canopic jars.

First put the stomach, liver, lungs
and intestines into some **natron salt**.
Leave them until they are dry.

Now brush them with **resin** and carefully
wrap them separately in strips of **linen**.

Place each bundle into its canopic jar.

LEAVE THE BODY TO

YOU WILL NEED

✓ **NATRON SALT**

✓ **SAWDUST**

✓ **A WAX PLATE**

✓ **SPICES**

✓ **JUNIPER BERRY OIL**

✓ **RESIN**

You now need to dry out the body so it will last for ever.

Pack natron salt inside and around the body. It will take forty days to dry out.

DRY

✓ **LINEN**

✓ **PALM OIL**

After forty days, take out the wet natron salt and stuff the body with clean linen and sawdust.

Rub some **spices** into the cut on the left side of the body and put a wax plate over it.

Now rub the skin with sweet smelling palm oil and **juniper berry** oil. This softens it and makes it smell better.

Finish by brushing the skin with resin.

WRAP THE BODY

Now wrap the body. This will take about fifteen days. You will need about twenty layers of linen. Linen fits better and lasts longer than wool.

Start with a sheet of linen big enough to knot above the head and below the feet.

Brush on resin glue between each layer of linen. The glue will stiffen the linen as it dries.

Wrap each finger and toe separately.

YOU WILL NEED
✓ **LINEN**

✓ **RESIN GLUE**

✓ **MAGIC CHARMS**

Then take a long strip of linen and criss-cross it around the head. Keep the strips of linen tight so that it keeps a good shape.

Place some lucky charms between the layers to keep the mummy safe and well.

MAKE THE MASK

YOU WILL NEED

✓ LINEN

✓ SCRAPS OF PAPYRUS

✓ SOME RESIN GLUE

✓ PAINTS AND BRUSHES

✓ GOLD LEAF

✓ A PAIR OF GLASS EYES

First you need to make a papier mâché mould. Take strips of linen and **papyrus** and lay them over the mummy's face.

To make the mask, smooth the layers down so they fit closely. Brush on resin glue between each layer.

Leave your mask to harden.

Once the mask is hard you can decorate it with paints and gold leaf.

Then paint the eyes and eyebrows in black. (Try to make the face as lifelike as possible so the spirit can recognise its mummy when it returns to the tomb.)

Now you are ready to fit the mask over the mummy's head.

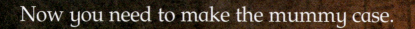 PREPARE THE MUMMY

Now you need to make the mummy case.

Make a case out of papier mâché by sticking strips of linen and papyrus together with resin.

The mummy should fit comfortably inside.

Now paint the case inside and out. On the inside, paint gods of the underworld like Nut, Thor, Osiris and Anubis.

YOU WILL NEED

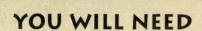

✓ **LINEN**

✓ **PAPYRUS**

✓ **RESIN**

CASE

On the outside, cover the mummy case with spells and **hieroglyphs** to help the spirit in the After Life.

Don't forget to paint on some eyes so the mummy can see out of the case. Make a door so the mummy can get out.

Brush on some gold leaf to decorate the case.

✓ PAINTS AND BRUSHES

MAKE A NEST OF CASE.

YOU WILL NEED

✓ AT LEAST FOUR
  WOODEN CASES,
  EACH SMALLER
  THAN THE LAST

The spirit has a dangerous journey to travel before it reaches the Kingdom of Osiris and the After Life. Keep it safe from tomb robbers and wild animals by making a nest of wooden mummy cases, each smaller than the last.

All the cases should fit inside one another, with the mummy in the smallest case. The mummy will then have lots of protection.

Paint the insides and outsides with spells and hieroglyphs and decorate with gold leaf and precious stones.

MAKE MODELS FOR

You need to make model workers who will help the spirit in the After Life. You need to make model workers for every task, including farm-workers, bakers, servants to fan the fire, and musicians to entertain at parties. You will also need working animals such as oxen for farming.

Mould the models from clay or wax or carve them from wood.

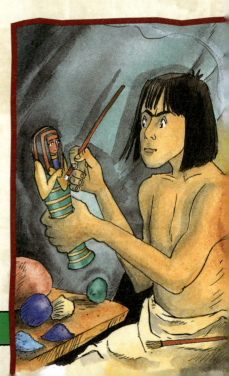

THE TOMB

YOU WILL NEED

✓ **MODELLING CLAY**

✓ **WOOD**

✓ **BRUSHES**

✓ **WAX**

✓ **PAINTS**

✓ **PAINTED BOXES**

Now paint them using brushes and paints to make them as lifelike as possible. Magic spells will bring them alive when they are needed in the After Life.

Pack them into painted boxes ready to go into the tomb.

You are now ready to decorate the tomb ready for the mummy.

Make the paintings on the walls as colourful and lively as possible to keep the mummy happy and entertained.

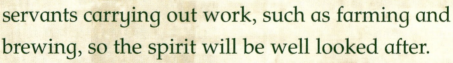

Include pictures of lots of activities, such as hunting and fishing, and parties, which the spirit will enjoy in the After Life. You also need to paint pictures of servants carrying out work, such as farming and brewing, so the spirit will be well looked after.

Write magic spells on the walls in hieroglyphs using a **reed** pen. The spells will make the wall pictures come to life when they are needed.

YOU WILL NEED

✓ ROPE BRUSHES AND PAPYRUS BRUSHES

✓ REED PENS

✓ PAINTS

MAKE SURE THE SPIRIT HA

The tomb must contain everything that the spirit will need in the After Life.

Leave plenty of food and drink, like bread, roast meat, baskets of fruit and jars of wine.

Arrange furniture, including a bed, a throne and a stool. A head rest will make the spirit more comfortable.

Put in extra clothes and jewellery and some board games for the spirit to play.

Now place the models of people and animals in the tomb. Say magic spells over them so that they will come alive and work for the spirit in the After Life.

YOU WILL NEED

✓ **A FUNERAL BIER**

✓ **TEAM OF OXEN**

✓ **DANCERS AND SINGERS**

✓ **PURE WATER**

✓ **MILK**

✓ **PRIEST**

✓ **PRIEST'S TOOLS**

You are now ready to carry the mummy to the tomb.

Place the mummy on a funeral **bier** and make sure you have enough oxen to pull it.

Organise some dancers and singers to perform as the mummy is carried to the tomb.

You will need a priest to carry out the ceremony which makes sure the mummy will be able to eat, drink and move around in the After Life. The priest will need some cups of pure water and milk to sprinkle on the mummy. Then he will need a special fork to touch the mummy's mouth so it will be able to speak in the After Life. He should now give the mummy a hug to welcome its soul to the After Life.

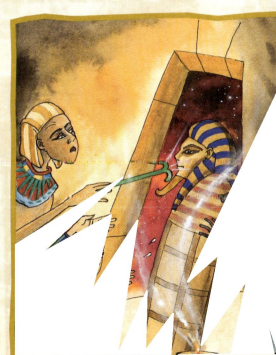

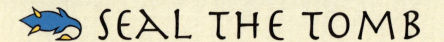 SEAL THE TOMB

 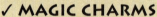   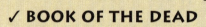 
Carry the mummy through the passage-ways to the burial chamber in the middle of the tomb.

Place magic charms and bricks around the mummy case. Don't forget to leave a *Book of the Dead* with maps and magic passwords to help the mummy in the After Life.

Now seal the door to the burial chamber with heavy blocks of stone to keep out tomb raiders. The entrance to the tomb should be well-hidden to keep the mummy safe inside.

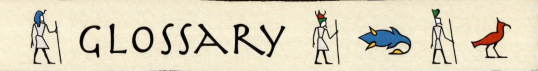

GLOSSARY

bier a funeral boat which was pulled on a sledge by a team of oxen

hieroglyphs a form of writing which uses tiny drawings of people, animals and objects

incense a mixture of gums and spices, burned to smell sweet

juniper berry fruit of juniper bushes or trees used to make sweet smelling oil

linen a type of material made from flax plants

natron salt a type of crusty salt found around lakes in the desert near Egypt

Nile water   water taken from the river Nile

palm oil and palm wine   oil and
wine made from the palm tree

papyrus   tall rush-like plants that grow on
marshes which are used to make a kind of
paper

reeds   plants with stiff hollow stems that grow
on marshes

resin   a type of gum taken from the
trunks of pine and fir trees

spices   plant extracts used for their smell,
flavour and medicinal qualities

INDEX